SECOND

HUMBLY
ASSISTING
THOSE IN
LEADERSHIP

L. E. ROMAINE

THE WORD
FOR TODAY

P.O. BOX 8000, COSTA MESA, CA 92628

SECOND
by L.E. Romaine
Published by **The Word for Today**
P.O. Box 8000, Costa Mesa, CA 92628
800 272-WORD (9673)
http://www.thewordfortoday.org

Copyright ©1996, 2004, 2006 by The Word for Today
Printed in the United States of America
ISBN 10: 0–936728–64-7
ISBN 13: 978-0–936728–64-3

Except where otherwise indicated, all Scripture quotations are taken from the King James Version of the Bible.

All rights reserved. No portion of this publication may be reproduced, stored in a retrieval system, or transmitted in any form or by any means without written consent of **The Word for Today.**

FROM • BECAUSE • THROUGH

The Lord Jesus Christ

The Holy Bible

A Lady named Ruth

A Man called Chuck

Scott

Laura

A Long-suffering Fellowship

Jan M., Debbie V., Cara T.

TABLE OF CONTENTS

1
THE REASON FOR WRITING THIS BOOK 1

2
ASSISTANT PASTOR 3

3
INGREDIENTS 11

4
SHADE 22

5
SENIOR PASTORS 33

6
PERSONAL 36

1

THE REASON FOR WRITING THIS BOOK

My hope in writing this book is that the new guys on the block may be jogged by something that is said, to give a kick to those that are resting on their laurels, and to remind some of how rich they are. This book spent some ten years in the thinking stage, nine of them in procrastination.

One day a fine lady waited to see me after a Bible study, and said simply, "You have a book in you." My reaction? I was boggled. No one, and I underline no one, was aware of the time I had spent considering a book concerning assistant pastors. Following this conversation, it

SECOND

seemed that I was consistently bombarded by people sharing similar thoughts. They would mention the need for something to be written on this subject.

On one such occasion a young man followed me around as I was closing up the church. It was New Year's Eve, around 1 a.m., and yet he wouldn't leave until he had told me how necessary a book of this kind was. I came to the conclusion that it was incumbent on somebody to deal with the more common mistakes that seem to follow the actions, duties, thoughts, and responsibilities of an assistant pastor. Having been one for years, and having in that time observed a vast horde of assistant pastors, I began to see the cracks and the chinks in the armor of serving.

Understand, that this is not intended to be a manual. It is simply a record of observations that have been made by folks in the fellowship, by other senior pastors, by other assistant pastors, by heathen, by the unsaved; and above all, by the one man that stands out among three great men in my life, my present senior pastor.

2

ASSISTANT PASTOR

The best working definition of the role of an assistant pastor can be seen in the relationships between Joshua and Moses in the Old Testament and also Timothy and Paul in the New Testament. I Corinthians 12:18 states, "But now hath God set the members every one of them in the body, as it hath pleased Him."

In the dictionary, it describes an assistant as one who backs up, undergirds and supports another. An assistant, by definition, is one who follows after another. In the church, the business of an assistant pastor is to complete the tasks the senior pastor cannot. With this in mind, an assistant has to be a man who takes

SECOND

initiative. A real assistant shouldn't be caught dead mumbling, "Oh, I didn't know…," "Nobody told me…," or "If I had known I would have." These are simply weak alibis that are so readily at hand for the inept. You have to *think*, you have to *look*, and then go *do*.

A self-starter is someone who doesn't have to be directed, or given sly innuendoes as to what could be done or should be done. He is someone, who by definition, is able to take off on his own and get things done. It is important to understand that in a self-starter, you have someone who is going to make a lot of errors and goofs. It must also be understood that the only person who makes mistakes is someone who is actually doing something. As an assistant you will overstep your boundaries. You will get out of your niche as you serve; you'll also get into areas that you don't belong, and you will find out very quickly that you need to back up. At that time, you will find out where your pride is, and how much humility and teachability you have when you are caught with egg on your face. If you are given specifics to do, don't under-do, and don't worry about over-doing.

ASSISTANT PASTOR

One of the greatest fallacies in ministry is the idea of a job description. As one young assistant pastor said to me, "You can give me eight hours of work to do and I'll get it done in three. Then I'll sit down and take it easy." <u>If you know the things that are expected of you, do them *as unto the Lord*. Don't look for strokes, pats and "atta boys" from men</u>. This is the junk that the world uses in order to get someone to do a job. In Matthew 6:5 we are told, "And when thou prayest, thou shalt not be as the hypocrites are." If you are looking for someone to pat you on the back or to compliment you when you serve, when they do, you have your reward.

For all seek their own, not the things which are Jesus Christ's. Finding a genuine assistant pastor is a rare thing. In Philippians 2:19–20, Paul said, "But I trust in the Lord Jesus to send Timothy shortly unto you, that I also may be of good comfort, when I know your state. For I have no man likeminded…." My, how that sits heavy. Even Paul had a hard time finding more than one good assistant. That is not to say that many don't start out on the right foot. Most assistant pastors are go-getters for the first six

SECOND

months. They're open for anything. They are in early and willing to stay late. Sometimes, miracle of miracles, they actually volunteer to stay late. They run to carry packages that are being brought into the church by ladies. They scoop up the wastebaskets in the office in a moment and they don't think that it's any big thing. But that again is in the first six months of the hire-in date. Given a small amount of additional time beyond that, you find that they go downhill. <u>They do less and less because they learn the system</u>. <u>They find out what they can get away with</u>, <u>what is allowed</u>, <u>and what is not allowed</u>. Within seven or eight months they start adjusting their schedules for their convenience. They ask the secretary to call up and cancel those people with appointments that might put them out. The result is that the secretaries have to listen to hurt people who were counting on that appointment to get help with a very serious problem. The needs of the people come last. The shame of it all, is when you go back and investigate some of these folks who "adjust" or rearrange their day, you find out that they had to go get their new car

ASSISTANT PASTOR

prepped before the warranty ran out, or they had to take Cousin Herman to the airport, and on and on ad nauseam.

They Have Learned The System. Did they start out that way? No. How did they end up that way? Because they're lazy. And sadly, once they have worked out what they can get away with and the bare minimum of what they can do, it's almost too late for input. Anything less than the threat of being fired or a pay cut doesn't wake them up. Even the strongest word of correction is a waste of time. What you get for your money is a short term spurt. Things will change for two days or two weeks but then they're back in the same rut that they were in before. I don't make this observation lightly. This is based upon years of watching assistant pastors.

There is only one cure for this sad situation. It is entirely necessary for you to encourage yourself in the Lord as an assistant pastor. When you show up on the grounds, show up early. You'll be surprised by what you find. In order to understand what is required of an assistant pastor, one must have an on-going commitment to being teachable. An assistant is

SECOND

not, I repeat, *not* nine-to-five. Some pastors have the reputation of being busy, but on observation you find that they are busy comparing notes on various computer gadgets and software. They will stand around and talk among themselves about baseball or football games while there are people waiting to be taken care of. They seem as though they couldn't care less, because they've already passed their six-month trial. The secretaries (those folks who really are the yeomen on the staff) will ask if anyone is available to minister to a person who has just walked in. I've seen situations with four pastors standing around. Three will look at one another and possibly the fourth will say, "I'll be glad to." That kind of attitude is hard to understand.

Another common pitfall for assistant pastors is man-pleasing. It is the most amazing thing to watch the movement and the talk and the jollies that come forward when the senior pastor shows up. They couldn't care less what the average person thinks or what God thinks, but they certainly don't want the senior pastor to think badly of them. If you say anything to these pastors, who are standing around, they

ASSISTANT PASTOR

become indignant. Suddenly, they start making jokes, being very glib and fast of mouth and quick of tongue. They will grasp for anything to take the heat off of themselves. They are embarrassed, and well, they should be. Somebody pointed out to them that they are here to serve, not to stand around and indulge themselves. It is not nice to have somebody tell an assistant pastor to move. At that point these "servants" become very indignant and bent out of shape. Why? Mainly because they were reminded that they're supposed to be sitting in the lower station and in the lower seat. But in the bloatedness of their own egos, believing their own press clippings, they've come to believe that they are really something. They will deny this, of course, but what they *do* does not match what they *say*.

It doesn't take a genius to find ways to be a real servant. You've got phones ringing, trash to be taken out, a floor that needs to be vacuumed, lights to be turned off or on, a church to be closed, restrooms to be serviced. But sadly, the thinking is "Let's hire some people to do it." The fact of the matter is the room is already

SECOND

filled with "hired people." The pastors are not servants, but hirelings.

It is the people in the fellowship that pay the freight, including the salaries of the assistant pastors. These folks need to be served as Jesus Christ served them. Nothing less.

3

INGREDIENTS

Let's talk about the ingredients that go into the making of a second man. <u>An assistant pastor is there to support the senior pastor, full-on, full-out, without grumbling</u>. The assistant is there to take orders or even suggestions with eagerness. Whether the need is to clean toilets or to teach Bible studies, they are there to help. Who is an assistant supposed to help? Anyone. An assistant is not "on the clock." He is not a member of a "pastor's union." As an assistant, you are not the senior pastor's buddy. You are to leave after taking care of all the basic needs of the church and everything is done that needs to be done. This often will mean leaving the church grounds long after the senior pastor has

SECOND

gone home. You are to be a Timothy, someone who does not seek his own interests, but those of Jesus Christ.

<u>You are to be available</u>. God's choosing of a man is not limited to those who have passed through a Christian college or seminary. The fact of the matter is that God can use people from all different kinds of educational backgrounds. Paul, for instance, was a highly educated man, but God chose him to share a very simple message. As he said in 1 Corinthians 1:17; "For Christ sent me not to baptize, but to preach the gospel: *not with wisdom of words,* lest the cross of Christ should be made of none effect." Paul was an educated man, but God also chose Peter, who was a businessman. Peter even went back to that business while he was waiting for power to come upon him from on high. Luke was a doctor, John was a teenager, but God was able to use their differing backgrounds for His glory. Everything in your personal history, all of the things that you have garnered, either by education or experience—or even by osmosis— God is able to use. You need not be puffed up by

INGREDIENTS

that. In fact, Paul said that those in the ministry are the *"offscouring"* (1 Cor. 4:13) of the world. Offscouring is not the kind of thing to be puffed up about. In fact, it is another name for a bathtub ring. God isn't interested in promoting the ego of individuals; God is only interested in furthering His kingdom and prospering His people.

God can cause all kinds of experiences to effectively train us for ministry. As a young man my mother's brother used to take me hunting and fishing. He taught me to respect other people's property. When you hunted or fished on someone else's land, you took your trash with you when you left. I was taught to leave the livestock alone, and to be sure the gates to the property were locked when we left. In the military I learned the value of regimentation and hard, personal discipline. Discipline has some flexibility, but regimentation means you do it this way, no other way, and you do it right now. A regimented approach does not allow for any extra-curricular input. I learned some difficult lessons as a novice youth director. I was so effective that the church finally had to throw me out. I thought that it was a disaster, when in fact, it was a wonderful way for God to sandpaper my ego. My, how you do learn from experience.

<u>One of the most important lessons to learn as an assistant pastor is that the church of God does not need you.</u> You just happened to be selected and placed there by God because you're a failure. I Corinthians 1:27 tells us, "But God hath chosen the foolish things of the world to confound the wise." No one serves in ministry because they have "arrived" spiritually. It's the Holy Spirit's place to mold and shape you after the walk and person of Jesus Christ, the Lord and Savior. It is your part to be flexible, available, and open to whatever molding the Lord chooses to do.

I sit under the leadership of a man who has over forty years in the ministry and has both discipline and a great love for God and personal freedom. Because of that, he leaves other people free to perform and to minister. He does not outline the work day for you. That is pretty heavy, this freedom stuff. But after awhile it becomes clear that freedom carries

INGREDIENTS

with it a large measure of responsibility.

This man, above everything else, has a tremendous interest and grasp of the Word of God. He's not interested in much of anything else, including administration and the other duties we usually assume go with the position of senior pastor. If something will help further the Kingdom of God, he's for it. You can learn a lot from such a teacher.

The one that is teaching me is Christ, and Christ is using my senior pastor, in turn, to teach me. I receive then double-tutoring. It is through him that I am being taught these things of God. I have not yet "apprehended" them as Paul says.

In fact, Paul said, "I have not attained, or am already perfected, but I press on that I may lay hold of that for which Jesus Christ has also laid hold of me. Brethren, I do not count myself to have apprehended: but one thing I do, forgetting those things which are behind and reaching forward to those things which are ahead, I press toward the goal for the prize of the upward call of God in Christ Jesus" (Philippians 3:12–14). This hunger to grow

SECOND

should be characteristic of every assistant pastor.

<u>The preparation for the ministry is the Word of God</u>. Most pastors and assistant pastors will so readily nod their heads to this, but it's not always true in their personal lives. Many assistant pastors believe the lie "because they prepare Bible studies then they are in the Word of God personally." It is absolutely crucial to make time to sit down with His Word, the Holy Bible, and just read it. Not to *do* a Bible study, not to analyze Greek words, not to pour over commentaries, but simply to sit down and read God's Word. We must read it like any of the saints read the Old or New Testaments. Just read it. In so doing, you are in fellowship with God. During this time He gets to talk to you. He's talking, and miracle of miracles, you're listening. If you are humbled, you are then teachable. Make it your business and establish your heart each day, fresh and new with God. If you are married, sit down with your wife and your Bible the *first thing in the morning.* Make Ephesians 5:25–28 the foundation of your marriage.

INGREDIENTS

The Holy Spirit came to establish us in the Word of God. He came to comfort, empower, and to teach you all things (John 14:26).

If you are in God's Word personally every morning, you will have good fellowship with Jehovah God and His Son Jesus Christ. If you are insistent through hunger and thirst that God would give you understanding concerning His Word, then you have fellowship with Him. It then follows that being a good husband, father, and pastor will be a snap because God will strengthen you in the inner man. God said that He would magnify His Word above His Holy name (Psalm 138:2). If then indeed He thinks that much of His Word, we had better give it the same value in both our private and family lives.

Quite often I will ask pastors if they read the Bible with their wives. They look at you as though you just arrived from the moon. Yet they'll go to church, and the fellowship will gather and they'll teach them the Word of God. But isn't it quite hypocritical that they don't have the same taste for the Word of God personally, and with their family, but they exhort and encourage others in the body of

SECOND

believers? I have heard many pastors exhort the body to search, learn, and to fall more in love with God as they know His Word. Doesn't it then stand to reason that you need to be doing the same as a man and with your family? God has called you to be responsible in all things.

According to 1 Timothy 5:8, you are to supply all of the needs of the family including the spiritual. You are the head, but not a dictator. We are to lead by example. This kind of leadership doesn't happen just in prayer meetings and Bible studies. Your family needs to know that they have a godly man in the house, not a preacher or a pastor, but a godly man who is an example as a father and as a husband. The results will blow your mind.

In 1 Peter 5:1–4, Peter declared, "The elders which are among you I exhort, who am also an elder, and a witness of the sufferings of Christ, and also a partaker of the glory that shall be revealed: Feed the flock of God which is among you, taking the oversight thereof, not by constraint, but willingly; not for filthy lucre, but of a ready mind; neither as being lords over God's heritage, but being examples to the flock.

INGREDIENTS

And when the Chief Shepherd shall appear, ye shall receive a crown of glory that fadeth not away." There are a number of warnings here that need to be taken seriously.

I have had firsthand experience with assistant pastors that have been utterly destroyed by money. Two additional things that will destroy a pastor are pride and illicit relationships with women. And whatever you do, don't look askance at others who fall. You had better be very careful of your own walk before God. You've got your hands full if you're doing it the way He wants. If you're truly following Jesus, you won't have much time to backbite or tear down someone else's walk. And when you slander someone else by talking about them behind their back, where is the scriptural justification for that?

You are in the ministry, not under constraint (because you were forced into it) and you're not there for money. You're to be ready (that means available) and with an open mind. If our hearts are right with God, we won't find ourselves cozening when five o'clock comes, burning rubber out of the parking lot.

SECOND

Equally important to keep in mind is 1 Peter 5:3, "Neither as being lords over God's heritage, but being examples to the flock." The book of James says, "My brethren, be not many masters, knowing that we shall receive the greater condemnation." God's standards for service are tough, and that's the way it's supposed to be.

No matter where you find yourself in life, up front where everyone can see you, or out on the street, know you are to be an example, constantly being willing to serve. These are the qualities God desires to see in the elders of the church. Don't look for money, don't look for raises. If you're having a hard time with the money crunch, look at your lifestyle. Pray with your wife. Take a look at your family finances. Then hearken back to the fact that you're telling other people that God has said to trust Him for every need out of His riches in glory by Christ Jesus (Phil. 4:19).

Doesn't it stand to reason that God expects you to do the same thing that you tell other people to do? Trust Him! Anything less than that is a sham. Peter said you are not to be "lords over God's heritage." Don't look down

INGREDIENTS

your nose at anyone. What gave you the idea you were elevated over others? Who put you in the seat of judgment? The only One who is allowed to do that is God Himself. He did not appoint you to do that. Did Jesus Christ look down on others? Was He too busy to serve? Then it behooves you in that measure to be Christ-like. If you don't have time to clean up the sanctuary, set up chairs—or know where the broom, the brush or the toilet plunger are—give me one good reason why you don't.

Busier men than you or me find time to serve. My senior pastor had just finished three services on a Sunday morning, when some folks came looking for him. I went to hunt him down and found him wading around in the men's restroom with his suit, tie, and shoes still on. One of the urinals in the men's restroom had overflowed and he was in there taking care of it. Don't be afraid to get dirty. Don't think for a minute that you are called to be lords over God's heritage. Don't think you are something when you're not. If you get puffed up, God has a way of sticking a pin in your balloon. You're to be an example.

4

SHADE

There are those who are appointed to labor in that place in the body called "the shade." They are not out where everyone can see them, they serve in a secondary role. To keep the church moving in power, we need both up-front and behind-the-scenes servants of God. These men that labor in the shade produce fruit that shall be richly accounted to them at the time of Christ.

At His coming they shall receive their reward. As Peter said, "And when the Chief Shepherd shall appear, ye shall receive a crown of glory that fadeth not away." And so it is with those who labor in the shade.

SHADE

There are few better examples of behind-the-scenes service than Andrew, who brought Peter to Jesus. After this great introduction, you hear more about Peter than Andrew—but where does Andrew stand in the eyes and the heart of our Lord? There was a Sunday School teacher in Mount Vernon who had a burden for a young man in his Sunday School class. That young man's name was Dwight Moody. We all know how God used Moody. But who was the Sunday School teacher and where does he stand in God's kingdom? Barnabas backed Paul and gave him credence in the face of fear and hatred. The focus of the book of Acts is on Paul, but who gave Paul his start? Who gave the sermon that arrested the attention of Charles Spurgeon? Both kinds of service, in the spotlight and in the shade, are blessed by the same Lord.

One Sunday, Charles Spurgeon was stuck in traffic and late to speak at a packed Cathedral. The leaders asked Spurgeon's father to speak in his son's place. When Charles Spurgeon arrived, his father handed the pulpit over to him, but not before he said the following words, "You came to hear my son and not me. I tell you

SECOND

that he can preach the gospel better than I, yet he has no better gospel to preach than I." Spurgeon's father was a man who knew who he was in the eyes of God, but more importantly he knew the gospel itself was more important than the one who shares it.

God desires for us to be about the business of bringing others to the Lord; for the one brought, as well as the person who brings are ever so precious in His sight. These are examples of laboring in the shade. There is a special kind of fruit that is only produced in the shade. The ongoing, overflowing joy of picking-up-after and going-in-behind produces a precious fruit for Jesus. And if God never shoves you forward, you are blessed out of your gourd. Rejoice that you are allowed that place in His kingdom.

In 1 Corinthians 12:22–23, the Bible says, "Nay, much more those members of the body, which seem to be more feeble, are necessary: and those members of the body which we think to be less honourable, upon these we bestow more abundant honour and our uncomely parts have more abundant comeliness." A true assistant pastor knows the more feeble ministries are necessary. An assistant pastor who fixes overflowing bathrooms and does it without fanfare or show is precious in God's sight.

Contrast that to those who find themselves well-satisfied with their position. In the book of Malachi our Lord is speaking in the closing pages of the Old Testament. It is both poignant and ironic that our Lord takes time out to correct the priests (or pastors) in the house of God. In Malachi 1:6 we read, "A son honoureth his father, and a servant his master: if then I be a father, where is mine honour? And if I be a master, where is my fear? Saith the Lord of Hosts unto you, O priests, that despise My Name. And ye say, wherein have we despised Thy Name?" The arrogant attitude we see in this verse can only come from someone who believes that his position is secure on the payroll.

In chapter 1, verse 7, God answers their flippant question by saying, "You offer polluted bread on My altar and you say, wherein have we polluted Thee? In that you say, the table of the Lord is contemptible." These "servants" were no longer concerned with the things that were offered to God. They were no longer concerned with the things that please God or displease God. They no longer received rebuke, not even from God. What a pathetic situation; yet, God says that it's true. And sadly enough, if they did it in Malachi, God's servants can do it in this day and age.

The nature of those who serve God doesn't change. They serve God on His terms and keep their commitment to Him. They want God to strengthen them, to keep them, and encourage them through the power of His Holy Spirit to serve. It isn't anything that they bring of themselves. But in our day, as in the day of Malachi, there is no longer any concern for quality control. The little things become contemptible. And yet our greatest sins begin with what seem like very small departures from God's standards.

In verse 8 of the same chapter the Lord said, "and if ye offer the blind for sacrifice, is it not evil? And if ye offer the lame and sick, is it not evil? Offer it now unto thy governor; will he be pleased with thee, or accept thy person? Saith the Lord of hosts." The priests allowed "seconds" to come into the house of God because they cared more about man's opinion than God's.

God says to them in verse 9, "And now, I pray you, beseech God that He will be gracious unto us: this hath been by your means: Will He regard your persons? saith the Lord of hosts." <u>Serving God's people in Jesus' name is a great privilege. Is</u> <u>that how you see it or has it become a burden and an obligation?</u> These are tough words, but God gets even tougher.

Look at verse 10, "Who is there even among you that would shut the doors for nought? Neither do ye kindle fire on mine altar for nought. I have no pleasure in you, saith the Lord of hosts, neither will I accept an offering at your hand." This is not some man's idea of serving God, nor is it negative just to be negative. This is not a case of someone looking at the hole in the donut. This is Jehovah God speaking to those who are supposed to be serving Him and leading the people by example.

SECOND

Again I say, read the reference for yourself for God said, "Unless you are paid you will not shut the doors of the temple." Once again we are faced with the temptations of being a hireling, serving God for profit. A man far wiser than I, pointed out to me that prosperity in ministry has ruined many men. As God blesses, they begin to raise their standard of living in proportion. They lose a sense of balance and they no longer are acquainted with the things of the sheep, for they live better than the people in the flock. The ministry suffers because these pastors have interests that go to other places and other things. This is sad. God is saying, "You no longer care about what is set before me."

In effect He said, "You are now a union pastor. You have stipulated duties and just get by. You didn't come in that way, but that's where you are now. If you started out in that first love to serve the Lord, how did you suddenly become hourly? Would you have ever said, "It's not my ministry," when you first began to serve the Lord? You did not arrive at this juncture overnight. You slipped away on a daily basis. You came to require less and less of yourself. It is a thing that's observable. I've seen it happen in my own life. Just as surely as I look at those Scriptures, I look at myself. I am to judge my own performance. Is it where God wants me? Who am I trying to please? Am I trying to please anyone but God?

Does it become kind of a cliched piece of conversation to say that you are well-pleasing unto God? Do we justify ourselves with statements like, "Well you don't know how much I study, brother." or "You're judging me." or any other slipshod method of excusing ourselves? Suddenly you require less and less of yourself and become a tragedy. God states that He is mocked at such a time. In Malachi God says, "My name is respected more among the heathen."

In chapter 2, we see some very pointed words for those who serve in the church. "And now, O ye priests, this commandment is for you. If ye will not hear, and if ye will not lay it to heart, to give glory unto my name, saith the Lord of hosts, I will even send a curse upon you, and I will curse your blessings: yea, I have

SECOND

cursed them already, because ye do not lay it to heart...For the priest's lips should keep knowledge, and they should seek the law at his mouth: for he is the messenger of the Lord of hosts."

Don't shame God by believing that you labor in a flourishing fellowship, and thereby take your comfort and ease. That's exactly what happened to these priests. They were secure in the idea that they were priests and their very position gave them security. They mistook the praise of man for the acceptance of God!

Be careful that you are not concerned with the title "pastor." A pastor is someone who takes care of the sheep as God directs. How we serve God shouldn't change simply because the fellowship is flourishing. If you are really in a balanced position before God in your heart, then you'll see all the people that you can see and you'll do all the things that need to be done. Now there are limits to this because you're only going to be able to do so much in one day. You're only going to see just so many people, but we should be open to fulfilling whatever opportunities before us to serve the Lord.

In Acts 2:46–47, we are told that the church flourished by breaking bread and fellowshipping together. God added daily to the church such as should be saved. Notice that it was God that added to the church such as should be saved. It's God's idea to add to the church. We can't take credit for this because God can remove us tomorrow. He decides if that fellowship will continue. He will add daily to it, so it doesn't depend upon our efforts. It never has and it never will. Understanding this forces us again to look at our own hearts. This is what God is concerned about.

Hebrews 4:13 tells us, "Neither is there any creature that is not manifest in His sight: but all things are naked and opened unto the eyes of Him with whom we have to do." Your performance as an assistant is open before Him.

Psalm 139:2 tells us that "He knows your thoughts from afar off." He also knows whether your service to Him is shabby or excellent, whether it is unto Him or for a paycheck, or to win the approval of some man. Read it again! Again, go back and look at it. These things are for you. God has stated that the church is composed

SECOND

of people who are purchased by His shed blood.

In Malachi 2:7, that incredible prophet speaking for God said that "A priest's lips should keep knowledge." That means that he should speak God's words as God's representative. Our public conduct should also match our message. But over and above that, you labor under the umbrella of the mercy of the openhanded gift of God who allows you the breath of life from day to day.

As you examine this section of Malachi, learn from our Lord and Father of our Savior. After these words in Malachi, God would not speak again for nearly 400 years. It would behoove you and me to think on this with a sober heart, as He admonishes His servants who labor in His house.

5

SENIOR PASTORS

HONOR HIS POSITION:
I CORINTHIANS 4:15

For though ye have ten thousand instructors in Christ, yet have ye not many fathers: for in Christ Jesus I have begotten you through the gospel.

You are to honor the position of the senior pastor as apportioned to him by God. Scripturally, the reason that you are to honor his position is because he is set for the saving of souls and he is a messenger of the Lord of hosts.

HONOR HIS WORK:
I THESSALONIANS 5:12-13

And we beseech you, brethren, to know them which labor among you, and are over

SECOND

you in the Lord, and admonish you; And to esteem them very highly in love for their work's sake. And be at peace among yourselves.

HONOR BY SUPPORT:
I TIMOTHY 5:19

Against an elder receive not an accusation, but before two or three witnesses.

You are to vindicate his position; you are to wipe out unjust criticisms. You do not support cheap shots. The understanding of that means you are a supporter of those uncalled criticisms of the senior pastor when you don't immediately seek to stop or rebuke them. If you let such slide by, you are then a partner with the gainsayer in stealing from the ministry and from the pastor's reputation. An example of what happens when somebody decides to rebuke one of God's chosen is found in Scripture (Numbers 12:1-10). God records that Aaron and Miriam sought to find fault with Moses. God's answer was that Miriam was struck with leprosy, and you can imagine Aaron's fright.

SENIOR PASTORS

HONOR HIS DOCTRINE:
II Corinthians 6:3

Giving no offense in any thing, that the ministry be not blamed.

You are to honor the senior pastor's doctrine. Disagreement is a reproach to the ministry. Division left unrepented, grows bitterness. The singleness of heart and accord in doctrine gives the fellowship a sound and a solid footing and Jesus Christ is honored.

HONOR BY WORD AND DEED:
I Peter 2:18-20

Servants, be subject to your masters with all fear; not only to the good and gentle, but also to the froward. For this is thankworthy, if a man for conscience toward God endure grief, suffering wrongfully. For what glory is it, if, when ye be buffeted for your faults, ye shall take it patiently? But if when ye do well, and suffer for it, ye take it patiently, this is acceptable with God.

6

PERSONAL

I PETER 1:12-15

Unto whom it was revealed, that not unto themselves, but unto us they did minister the things, which are now reported unto you by them that have preached the gospel unto you with the Holy Ghost sent down from heaven; which things the angels desire to look into. Wherefore gird up the loins of your mind, be sober, and hope to the end for the grace that is to be brought unto you at the revelation of Jesus Christ. As obedient children, not fashioning yourselves according to the former lusts in your ignorance: But as He which hath called you is holy, so be ye holy in all manner of conversation....

The preceding Scripture is the idea behind

PERSONAL

these pages, and my purpose scripturally for writing these notes.

I PETER 1:2

Elect according to the foreknowledge of God the Father, through sanctification of the Spirit, unto obedience and sprinkling of the blood of Jesus Christ: Grace unto you, and peace, be multiplied.

I PETER 1:4-8

To an inheritance incorruptible, and undefiled, and that fadeth not away, reserved in heaven for you, Who are kept by the power of God through faith unto salvation ready to be revealed in the last time. Wherein ye greatly rejoice, though now for a season, if need be, ye are in heaviness through manifold temptations: That the trial of your faith, being much more precious than of gold that perisheth, though it be tried with fire, might be found unto praise and honour and glory at the appearing of Jesus Christ: Whom having not seen, ye love; in whom, though now ye see Him not, yet believing, ye rejoice with joy unspeakable and full of glory.

Take heart. Peter failed at walking on the water, in the garden, and at the crucifixion. Listen to this man. He now knows who he is and where he is going. He now speaks of rejoicing and trials. His end is that he now speaks of love. How is this change possible? It is possible because, as he says in verse 2 of the Scripture reference, that he is sprinkled with the blood of Christ. That's why he can rejoice. That's why he's changed. That's why his failures can be put behind him because he knows who he is and how precious and how costly he is. The same is true for you.

PSALM 71:7-9

> I am as a wonder unto many; but Thou art my strong refuge. Let my mouth be filled with Thy praise and with Thy honor all the day. Cast me not off in the time of old age; forsake me not when my strength faileth.

PSALM 71:18

> Now also when I am old and grayheaded, O God, forsake me not; until I have shewed Thy strength unto this generation, and thy power to every one that is to come.

OTHERS MAY, YOU CANNOT

G. D. Watson, 1845-1924, was a Wesleyan Methodist Minister and Evangelist based in Los Angeles, California. His Evangelistic campaigns took him to England, the West Indies, New Zealand, Australia, Japan, and Korea. He also wrote several books. This article was originally published in pamphlet form.

IF GOD HAS CALLED YOU to be really like Jesus, He will draw you to a life of crucifixion and humility, and put upon you such demands of obedience, that you will not be able to follow other people or measure yourself by other Christians, and in many ways He will seem to let other good people do things which He will not let you do.

OTHER CHRISTIANS and ministers who seem very religious and useful may push themselves, pull wires, and work schemes to carry out their plans, but you cannot do it, and if you attempt it you will meet with such failure and rebuke from the Lord as to make you sorely penitent.

OTHERS MAY BOAST of themselves, of their work, of their success of their writings, but the Holy Spirit will not allow you to do any such thing, and if you begin it, He will lead you into some deep mortification that will make you despise yourself and all your good works.

OTHERS MAY BE ALLOWED to succeed in making money, or may have a legacy left to them, but it is likely God will keep you poor, because He wants you to have something far better than gold, namely, a helpless dependence on Him, that He may have the privilege of supplying your needs day by day out of any unseen treasury.

THE LORD MAY LET OTHERS be honored and put

forward, and keep you hidden in obscurity, because He wants you to produce some choice, fragrant fruit for His coming glory, which can only be produced in the shade. He may let others be great, but keep you small. He may let others do a work for Him and get the credit of it, but He will make you toil on without knowing how much you are doing; and then to make your work still more precious, He may let others get the credit for the work which you have done, and thus, make your reward ten times greater when Jesus comes.

THE HOLY SPIRIT will put a strict watch over you, with a jealous love, and will rebuke you for little words and feelings, or for wasting your time, which other Christians never seem distressed over. So make up your mind that God is an infinite Sovereign, and has a right to do as He pleases with His own.

HE MAY NOT EXPLAIN to you a thousand things which will puzzle your reason in His dealings with you. But if you absolutely sell yourself to be His… slave, He will wrap you up in a jealous love, and bestow upon you many blessings which will come only to those who are in the inner circle.

SETTLE IT FOREVER, then, that you are to deal directly with the Holy Spirit, and that He is to have the privilege of tying your tongue, or chaining your hand, or closing your eyes, in ways that He does not seem to use with others. Now when you are so possessed with the Living God that you are, in your secret heart, pleased and delighted over this peculiar, personal, private, jealous guardianship and management of the Holy Spirit over your life, you will have found the vestibule of Heaven.